THE LITTLE BOOK OF CHOCOLAT

JOANNE HARRIS

THE LITTLE BOOK OF

CHOCOLAT

AND FRAN WARDE

Doubleday

LONDON · NEW YORK · TORONTO · SYDNEY · AUCKLAND

TRANSWORLD PUBLISHERS
61–63 Uxbridge Road, London W5 5SA
A Random House Group Company
www.transworldbooks.co.uk

First published in Great Britain
in 2014 by Doubleday
an imprint of Transworld Publishers

A CIP catalogue record for this book
is available from the British Library.

ISBN 9780857522009

Addresses for Random House Group Ltd companies outside the UK
can be found at: www.randomhouse.co.uk
The Random House Group Ltd Reg. No. 954009

The Random House Group Limited supports the Forest Stewardship Council® (FSC®), the leading
international forest-certification organisation. Our books carrying the FSC label are printed on
FSC®-certified paper. FSC is the only forest-certification scheme supported by the leading environmental organisations,
including Greenpeace. Our paper procurement policy can be found at www.randomhouse.co.uk/environment

Photography: all images by Philip Webb except pages 55 and 126 © Johnny Ring
Food styling: Fran Warde
Props: Pene Parker
Design: Lisa Horton

Printed and bound in Germany

2 4 6 8 10 9 7 5 3 1

To chocoholics around
the world

x

CONTENTS

INTRODUCTION

Back in 1998, when I started to write a little book called *Chocolat* – my third book, and something of a departure from the Gothic pastiches I'd written before – I was completely unaware of the genie I was about to release into my ordered little world. My story, a light-hearted fable set in a not-quite-current France, had as its central metaphor the concept of food as redemption – food, and most precisely, chocolate.

Why chocolate, do you ask? Why not cheese, or chillies, or olives, or bread? I am not a chocoholic: although I do enjoy chocolate occasionally, it's not among the foods that I could never live without (for that, see the chillies and cheese above). And yet, as I wrote my story, I found myself increasingly fascinated by the history and folklore of chocolate; its capacity to transform and evolve; and, of course, the emotional resonance that chocolate holds for so many of us, something that transcends mere taste and becomes a spiritual journey.

I was born in a sweet-shop. A corner sweet-shop in Barnsley, to be precise; a place as far removed from Vianne Rocher's elegant little *chocolaterie* as it was possible to be. The shop, which belonged to my grandparents, sold mostly newspapers and sweets, the sweets in glass jars in the window, kaleidoscopic and fascinating. I very rarely ate any. Chocolate, too, was a rare treat – and, at that time, generally not of wonderful quality. The kind of boutique chocolate shops that now inhabit the high street were altogether unknown – except perhaps in London – and the occasional trip to Thorntons was a very special pilgrimage.

But on my trips to France to visit my French family – trips that coincided with my school holidays – the story was very different. At Easter, in particular, every *confiserie* – that word which translates as 'confectioner' but which holds a wealth of other associations, and which the French high street finds as indispensable as any bakery – was filled with Easter chocolates.

Of course, we had Easter eggs in England. But ours were dull in comparison – gritty, fatty chocolate in foil and cardboard, while the French ones were works of art, wrapped in transparent cellophane, their natural gloss shining through, tied with artfully curled ribbons and decorated with clusters of flowers and fruit, cleverly piped on in icing sugar. Others were made of brightly coloured papier-mâché, painted with traditional designs and filled with tiny chocolate shapes. Some were small enough to be sold at pocket-money prices; others were large enough to qualify as sculpture, each confectioner vying with his rivals to create bigger, better, more beautiful pieces.

And the French confectioners did not limit their creativity to decorating eggs. There were also chocolate menageries of hens, rabbits, piglets, ducks – all symbols of prosperity – along with winged bells and paper cones filled with chocolates and toys, like pagan cornucopia. At the time, it seemed to me that this very Catholic country had retained far more of its ancient Easter rituals and images than England, although it could simply be that Catholicism has always had a natural capacity to assimilate and re-invent popular traditions.

Thus, when I was a child I was taught that the reason why church bells fall silent on Good Friday is that they magically leave their bell-towers, grow angel wings and fly – invisibly, upside-down – to Rome to be blessed by the Pope before Easter. The Pope's blessings take physical, magical form as chocolate figures – animals, eggs, and, of course, those winged bells – which fill the church bells as they fly home to ring on Easter Sunday. But as soon as the bells return to the church-towers and start to ring, the thousands of chocolate shapes they contain are flung out all over the countryside. The only way to collect them and stop them smashing on to the ground is to build a nest and to hide it in the branches of a tree, so that the chocolates land inside. On Easter Sunday, before setting off to church, French children still make nests to be filled with chocolate animals and collected after the service: Catholicism and paganism co-existing happily in a celebration of spring rebirth and spiritual regeneration.

And this was where *Chocolat* was born, between the beautiful chocolate shops of western France and the close little Yorkshire community that shaped so much of my childhood: a story, not just of chocolate, but of people living together in a place formed by traditions; of insiders and outsiders; of folklore and religion; tolerance and cruelty; feasting, fasting and family. At the time, I had no idea how far that story was to take me. It gave me wings – just like those bells – and sent me all around the world. A story can sometimes do that, you know: and quite unexpectedly, *Chocolat* had become one of those stories, linking me with readers from over fifty countries, sending me to Hollywood, boosting me out of my orbit into a new, extraordinary life.

It was the first time I'd really considered the magical powers of chocolate. Papal blessings aside, I was used to thinking of chocolate as a delicious indulgence rather than the stuff of dreams. And yet, there is a real magic to this ancient, mysterious substance. After all, the history of chocolate predates Christianity. There is evidence to suggest that it was used over 2,500 years ago in Central America, where the Olmec were probably the first consumers. The Olmec were a fascinating people – deeply spiritual, sophisticated, scientific, artistic – and though we still know too little about them, we do know that they used chocolate, although they ground the beans to make a strong, bitter drink very different to the kind of hot chocolate we enjoy today.

The Olmec created a solid foundation for the later Mesoamerican cultures – the Maya and the Aztecs. Certainly, by the time the Maya took over from the Olmec, chocolate – or *cacahuatl* ('bitter water') – had become more than just a drink. It was prized as a health food, a stimulant and a divine gift, and its preparation was increasingly ritualized. Mixed with cornmeal, water, chilli, vanilla, honey and spices, the first chocolate drink was red, not brown, and was probably served hot. These people also used chocolate as a condiment – perhaps something like the mole sauce still used in Mexican cooking.

Most importantly, the Maya venerated chocolate as a divine gift from the goddess Ixcacao, who gave the first cocoa tree to mankind. In other Mayan mythologies, Ixcacao was married against her will to Ek Chua, the trader god, who turned her divine gift of cacao into currency; a currency that endured in some parts of Latin America into the nineteenth century. From their uneasy union came a war

between chocolate's spiritual and commercial aspects; a war still fought today in the Western world, between those who feel that Easter should be a time of spiritual contemplation, and those who simply want to eat as much chocolate as they can.

After the collapse of the Mayan culture came the Aztecs, who also used chocolate as currency. A tomato was worth 1 cacao bean; a night with a prostitute, 10 beans; the price of a slave, 100 beans. Stores of counterfeit beans have been found – even then people were prepared to cheat the system. Now a commercial enterprise, chocolate was the privilege of the elite: leaders, priests, warriors and officials.

The Aztecs also seem to have lived in a state of perpetual fear of sin, or offending any one of their many hostile deities. The land of chocolate had become a land of fear and nightmare, and when Cortez arrived in the New World, he was quick to exploit such local beliefs – especially the legend that the god Quetzalcoatl would one day return to Earth as a fair-skinned, bearded man. Emperor Montezuma assumed that Cortez and his people were gods – or at the very least, their envoys.

I suppose this is where the second book in my *Chocolat* series was born: in the time of blood and chocolate. My villain, Zozie de l'Alba, is a representation of this inheritance – the dark side of chocolate, if you like. Today, of course, it's hard to believe that chocolate ever had a dark side. And as I learnt more about it – some as research for *Chocolat*, but much more after the book had come out, as kindred spirits all over the world were impelled to share their experiences and to add their voices to the growing number of people my story had inspired – I realized that there's a lot more to chocolate than Easter eggs, or chocolate bars, or Cadbury's chocolate animals. We tend to take it for granted now; chocolate has become an everyday indulgence, and as our taste for it has grown, the range of flavours and quality has also grown accordingly. But the story of chocolate has a magic of its own and, in spite of its popularity, the world's favourite flavour still retains some of its ancient mysteries. Perhaps you'll discover a few of them in the pages of this book. Or perhaps you'd rather just indulge. Either way, it's all right.

Joanne Harris
December 2013

FRAN'S CHOCOLATE TIPS

All chocolate is produced in warm countries within approximately ten and twenty degrees either side of the equator. The cocoa beans are picked, fermented and dried in the country of source but are then transported to Europe or the USA to be manufactured into chocolate, although some small and unique artisan producers grow and produce chocolate in the country of origin.

Chocolate is as complex and alluring as wine. Its distinctive taste is influenced by a host of different factors from the plant variety and the environment in which the bean grows to the fermentation, drying and final production processing. Chocolate's subtle flavours aren't always immediately obvious, but the more chocolate you taste, the more refined your chocolate palate will become. Treat yourself and visit a fine chocolate shop to put your taste buds to the test.

Dark chocolate will have a high percentage of cocoa solids and a low amount of sugar.

Milk chocolate will have added sugar and either condensed milk or milk 'crumb', which is a caramelized powder.

Cheaper chocolates will have been bulked out with vegetable fats and usually have a much higher sugar content, meaning the cocoa solid content is lowered.

White chocolate actually contains no cocoa solids, but good white chocolate will be made with 100% cocoa butter. Steer clear of any made with vegetable fat.

Tempering Chocolate

This is a complicated but essential art if you want to produce shiny, smooth chocolate. When heated, the fat content of chocolate melts and is restructured into crystals – ideally, these crystals should be evenly sized to ensure a good firm texture and shiny surface when the chocolate is shaped and hardened. Unfortunately, incorrect tempering can mean that the crystals become irregular in size during solidifying, resulting in a dull chocolate. To keep the crystals even and to achieve perfect results, the chocolate must be tempered.

How to Temper Chocolate (see chart below for chocolate types)

Equipment

Heat-proof mixing bowl that fits snugly over a saucepan
Saucepan
Digital thermometer
Spatula

1. Break the chocolate into small, even sized pieces.
2. Place two thirds of the chocolate pieces in the heat-proof bowl.
3. Fill the saucepan with enough water to reach just below the bowl when placed on top. It must fit snugly so that the steam does not escape (this is known as a 'bain-marie').
4. Place on a medium heat to warm the water to a shivering simmer. Do not boil.
5. Melt the chocolate very slowly. Do not allow it to reach a temperature higher than the melting temperature (see chart below).
6. Once totally melted, remove the bowl, add the remaining chocolate and mix quickly with a spatula, until all the pieces have melted into the chocolate.
7. Leave the chocolate to cool to the crystallizing temperature (see chart below).
8. Return the bowl to the saucepan, mix continuously and allow the temperature to very gently return to the working temperature (see chart below).
9. Do not rush any of these stages and you will have perfectly tempered chocolate.

	Melting temperature	Crystallizing temperature	Working temperature
Dark Chocolate	55°C	27–28°C	31–32°C
Milk Chocolate	50–55°C	26–27°C	29–30°C
White Chocolate	50°C	26–27°C	29–30°C

'In glass bells and dishes lie the chocolates, the pralines, Venus's nipples, truffles, mendiants, candied fruit, hazelnut clusters . . .'

RECIPES

rose petals, sugared violets . . .

. . . they gleam darkly, like sunken treasure, Aladdin's cave of sweet clichés.'

QUETZALCOATL'S CHOCOLATE CAKE

According to ancient belief, Quetzalcoatl, the feathered serpent god of the Aztecs, was the lord of light and the harvest, as well as the inventor of books and the calendar. He was worshipped with chocolate and golden maize, which makes this twist on the classic Devil's Food Cake especially appropriate, relying as it does on the combination of butter, rich chocolate and golden syrup to give it a luscious consistency.

Takes 1½ hours / serves 8

butter for greasing tin
150g butter
150g unrefined light brown sugar
150g golden syrup
2 eggs, beaten
225ml milk

45g cocoa powder
225g plain flour
1½ tsp baking powder

Icing

4 tbsp cocoa powder
150g butter, soft
300g icing sugar
1½ tbsp golden syrup
3 drops vanilla extract

Heat the oven to 180°C/gas mark 4. Butter two 20cm sandwich tins and line the bases with baking parchment.

Place the butter, sugar and golden syrup in a saucepan over a low heat. Mix until melted and blended. Remove from the heat and cool for 5 minutes. Mix the egg and milk thoroughly in a bowl, before adding the contents of the saucepan and mixing thoroughly. Finally, fold in the cocoa, flour and baking powder.

Divide the mixture between the two prepared cake tins and smooth the top with a palette knife. Place in the middle of the oven and cook for 30 minutes. The mixture should have shrunk away from the sides of the tins a little and when a knife is inserted into the middle it should come out clean. Cool for 5 minutes and then turn the cake out on to a wire rack to cool.

To make the icing, mix the cocoa with the 4 tbsp of hot water in a bowl until smooth. Add the butter, icing sugar, golden syrup and vanilla extract and beat until smooth and creamy.

When the cakes are cold, sandwich them together with some of the icing. Spread the remainder over the top and sides of the cake. To help with spreading, dip your palette knife in hot water to stop the icing sticking to it, then work to your chosen finish, smooth or whirls.

LE MOCHA

This is the essential mocha – an irresistible blend of dark chocolate layered with espresso and fresh cream. A perfect way to start the day with a little sweet indulgence . . .

Takes 10 minutes / serves 2

2 shots espresso coffee
400ml full-fat milk
75g dark chocolate, grated
unrefined brown sugar, to taste
100ml whipped double cream
cocoa powder

Make two shots of espresso coffee (a Bialetti coffee pot works best for this). Heat the milk in a saucepan. Add the grated chocolate, a little sugar to taste and stir until completely melted.

Pour the hot chocolate into two heatproof glasses. Hold a spoon (rounded side up) over each glass and carefully pour in the espresso, then top with the whipped cream and a dusting of cocoa powder or a drizzle of melted chocolate. Serve with a long spoon, and enjoy.

The Mayans liked their chocolate hot and frothy, flavoured with chilli and vanilla, sculpting tubes into their pots so they could blow the liquid into a foam.

MONTEZUMA'S SHORTBREAD

These rich caramel chocolate squares are traditionally known as 'millionaire's shortbread'. Add a little edible gold leaf on top and even Montezuma, the Chocolate King, would approve . . .

Takes 2½ hours / makes 16

Shortbread
250g plain flour
80g unrefined caster sugar
200g butter

Salted caramel
100g butter
100g unrefined soft light
 brown sugar
2 x 397g cans condensed milk

Topping
250g dark chocolate, broken into
 small, even-sized pieces
2 tbsp golden syrup
100g butter

Heat the oven to 180°C/gas mark 4. Line a 33 x 25cm shallow tray with baking parchment.

In a food processor, blend the flour and caster sugar, then add the butter in small pieces, whizzing until it resembles fine breadcrumbs. Spread the mixture evenly on the lined tray, then compress it firmly with the palm of your hand or the back of a spoon. Place in the middle of the oven and bake for 25 minutes until just golden brown. Leave to cool in the tin.

To make the caramel, place the butter and sugar in a non-stick saucepan and heat very gently, stirring constantly until the sugar has dissolved. Add the condensed milk. Increase the heat, bring to a rapid boil, stirring continuously, and then reduce the heat and simmer for 5 minutes until the mixture has thickened. Quickly pour over the cooled shortbread in an even layer and chill until set.

For the topping, melt the chocolate, golden syrup and butter in a bain-marie and blend together. Pour over the cold caramel and spread with a large palette knife. Leave to cool and set. Cut into 16 squares.

Aztec Emperor Montezuma reportedly drank over fifty portions of chocolatl daily, calling it 'the divine drink'.

CHOCOLATE FUDGE SQUARES

Fudge, a sweet, rich compound of sugar, butter and milk, seems to have originated in America near the end of the nineteenth century. This chocolate fudge is easy to make, and is also great served warm, over ice cream.

Takes 1½ hours / makes 50 pieces

*400g dark or milk chocolate, broken into
   small, even-sized pieces*
25g butter
397g can condensed milk
100g icing sugar
30g cocoa powder, sifted

Line a 20cm square, shallow tin with baking parchment.

Melt the chocolate in a bain-marie. In a non-stick saucepan, melt the butter and gently warm the condensed milk, then add the melted chocolate and mix until smooth. Beat in the icing sugar until blended and smooth.

Put the mixture into the prepared tin, spread evenly into the corners, smooth over the top and place in the fridge to set for at least 1 hour. Remove and cut into small squares and dust with cocoa.

*Portuguese poet Fernando Pessoa once wrote
'There is no metaphysics on earth like chocolate'.*

SISTERS OF MERCY PROFITEROLES

It's no coincidence that in France the local pâtisserie often stands in front of the church. Perhaps the local curé needs to keep an eye on the opposition – or maybe he's just checking out what he wants for dessert. Either way, bishops, saints, apostles and nuns have always figured prominently in the pastry-chef's lexicon. These delicious little chocolate-mocha profiteroles are a reminder to all of us that to be forgiven, we first have to sin . . .

Takes 1 ½ hours / serves 6–8

Choux buns
85g butter, cut into small pieces
220ml water
110g plain flour
a pinch of salt
3 eggs, beaten

Filling
400ml double cream
2 tsp instant coffee

Sauce
100g dark chocolate, broken into
  small, even-sized pieces
1 tbsp golden syrup
50ml double cream

Heat the oven to 220°C/gas mark 7, and place a baking tray at the bottom of the oven. This will create the steam to help the buns rise. Line a large baking sheet with baking parchment.

Gently heat the butter and water in a medium saucepan, stirring constantly. When the liquid comes to a rapid boil, turn off the heat and add the flour and salt. Mix rapidly with a wooden spoon until the mixture comes away from the sides and is smooth. Leave to cool for 5 minutes, then add a little of the egg and beat until smooth. Add more egg a little at a time until it is all incorporated. The consistency should be smooth, shiny and stiff enough to hold its own shape.

Spoon sixteen large teaspoons of the mixture on to the baking sheet, leaving room for them to expand, then place in the middle of the oven. Quickly add 75ml water to the baking tray in the bottom of the oven and shut the door. Bake for 10–15 minutes. Reduce the oven temperature to 190°C/gas mark 5 and cook for a further 15–20 minutes until the buns are golden and crisp. Remove from the oven, make a small cut in the side of each one and cool on a cooling wire.

To make the filling, dissolve the coffee in a little hot water, then add to the cream in a bowl and whisk until it stands in peaks. Place in a nozzled piping bag and fill each choux bun. Make the sauce by melting the chocolate, syrup and cream in a bain-marie, mix until blended and then dip each choux bun in the chocolate.

P'TITE MÈRE'S CHOCOLATE CHESTNUT TRUFFLES

My French grandmother (or P'tite Mère, as we called her) hated all fruit and nuts except for chestnuts, which she adored. I think she would have enjoyed these chestnut truffles, combining as they do the earthy scent of autumn with the silky sophistication of chocolate . . .

Takes 2 hours / makes 50

200g dark chocolate, broken into
  small, even-sized pieces
100g chestnut purée
200g double cream
75g unrefined light brown sugar
25g cocoa powder

Line a baking tray approximately 20 x 16cm with baking parchment.

In a bain-marie, place the chocolate, chestnut purée, cream and sugar, and heat gently until melted. Then remove from the bain-marie and mix until evenly blended.

Place in the fridge until firmly set (at least 1 hour). When set, use a teaspoon to scoop out evenly sized balls and roll them between your palms one at a time.

Put the cocoa in a shallow bowl and toss each truffle in the powder. Repeat until all are coated. Store in an airtight container in the fridge for up to 1 week (assuming you can resist them for that long).

'The smell of chocolate is overwhelming . . . an exquisite trail of sweetness.'

MAPLE AND WALNUT CHOCOLATE ICE CREAM

Home-made ice cream is great fun to make, easy and very satisfying. This recipe is just one of the many ways in which chocolate can be used to dress up an old favourite – in this case giving the classic maple and walnut an elegant chocolate makeover.

Takes 2 hours / serves 6

60g walnuts, chopped
100ml maple syrup
300ml milk
4 egg yolks

a pinch of salt
150g dark chocolate, broken into
 small, even-sized pieces
200ml double cream

Place the walnuts and maple syrup in a small non-stick pan and gently heat over a medium heat for 5 minutes. Remove and leave to cool.

Heat the milk in a saucepan. Whisk the egg yolks and salt in a heatproof bowl, then pour in the warm milk and whisk. Make a bain-marie using this bowl and gently heat the egg mixture until it thickens enough to coat the back of a spoon (this will take about 7 minutes; don't try to rush it, as direct heat will curdle the mixture). Add the chocolate and stir into the mixture until melted, then remove from the bain-marie and chill.

Whip the cream into very soft peaks and blend into the mixture, then pour into an ice-cream maker and blend until almost frozen (follow machine instructions). Add the cooled maple-nut mix and churn through. Place in the freezer for 20 minutes to firm, or store in the freezer – but remember, always take out 20 minutes before serving so that it is soft enough for scooping.

An average chocolate bar contains around the same amount of antioxidants as a 140ml glass of red wine.

CHOCOLATE PUDDING FLEUR DE SEL

The French are not the only country to have had a love affair with puddings. The word 'pudding' originates from the French *boudin* – although this very English steamed pudding bears little resemblance to that. Here, the traditional steamed sponge is given a lovely twist with butter caramel and *fleur de sel* – the best comes from the island of Noirmoutier and has a characteristic violet scent, although any flaked sea salt will do just fine.

Takes 2½ hours / serves 6–8

Pudding
butter for greasing tin
100g dark chocolate, broken into
  small, even-sized pieces
150g butter, soft
150g unrefined caster sugar

3 eggs
25g cocoa powder
¼ tsp sea salt
150g self-raising flour
2 tbsp milk

Caramel sauce
75g butter
150g unrefined brown sugar
2 tbsp golden syrup
150ml double cream
a pinch of fleur de sel

Butter a 1kg pudding basin. (Be generous!) In a bain-marie, melt the chocolate. In a separate bowl, use an electric whisk to blend together the butter and sugar, add the eggs and whisk again. Pour in the melted chocolate, cocoa and sea salt, then whisk again until smooth. Fold in the flour, then stir in the milk and mix well until blended.

Put into the prepared pudding basin, cover with cling film and tie with string, making a handle to lift. Place in a large saucepan. Pour in enough hot water to come halfway up the side of the pudding basin, then place on the hob with a lid on and bring to the boil. Reduce heat and simmer gently for 1½–2 hours. Constantly check the water and add more if needed.

To make the sauce, melt the butter, sugar and golden syrup in a small saucepan over a low heat, stirring until smooth and bubbling. Add the cream and sea salt, stir, then set to one side.

Check if the pudding is cooked by inserting a knife in the centre – the blade should come out clean. Once cooked, remove the cling film and allow to sit for 5 minutes. Then, very carefully, run a palette knife around the edge and place a plate on the pudding basin; turn the basin over, shake and – fingers crossed – release the pudding on to the plate. Spoon over a little of the caramel, sprinkle with a few salt crystals and serve with the extra sauce in a jug.

CHOCOLATE-HEART MUFFINS

These pretty muffins contain an extra indulgence – a soft, chocolate-hazelnut cream centre.

Takes 1 hour, plus cooling / makes 6

30g cocoa powder
100ml hot water
150g butter
150g unrefined caster sugar
3 eggs
150g self-raising flour

Filling
75g Nutella chocolate spread
40g double cream

Heat oven to 180°C/gas mark 4.

Blend together the cocoa and hot water. Whisk together the butter and caster sugar until creamy, then add the eggs and beat well. Fold in the flour and dissolved cocoa, then mix evenly. For a truly authentic large muffin, divide the mixture between the six cups of a deep silicone muffin tray, and bake for 30 minutes in the middle of the oven.

Leave to cool for 5 minutes, then carefully remove the muffins from the tray and transfer on to a wire cooling rack. When cool, cut out a disc from the top of each cake.

To make the filling, gently warm the Nutella in a bain-marie, then add the cream and blend until smooth. Spoon a teaspoon of the mixture into the hole cut into each muffin, then gently replace the cut-out discs (don't squash them down). Dust with a little icing sugar.

*The melting point of cocoa butter is just below body temperature
– which is why it melts in your mouth.*

PETS D'ANGE

Meringues have existed under various names since the seventeenth century.
In the Loire region of France they are still sometimes known as *pets* or *pets
d'ange* (angel farts) for their fluffy, cloud-like consistency. They are doubly
angelic for being entirely fat-free – even a tiny trace of fat can cause the
beaten egg whites to collapse. For this reason, my grandmother always
wiped the mixing bowl with a piece of lemon before adding the egg whites
– although her explanation was more fanciful: she said that the lemon juice
was to squirt into the Devil's eye, to keep him out of the cooking . . .

Takes 4 hours / serves 6

4 large egg whites
200g unrefined caster sugar
10g cocoa powder

Heat the oven to 140°C/gas mark 1. Line a baking sheet with baking parchment.

Whisk the egg whites with an electric whisk until stiff and standing in peaks. Add half the
sugar, whisk again, then add the remaining sugar and whisk once more. Sieve in the cocoa
powder and stir just once with a metal spoon to create a marbled effect – it should not be too
evenly blended.

Spoon out on to the baking sheet into six large meringues. Place in the middle of the oven
and cook for 3 hours for gooey, soft middles – or, if you want the meringues dry all the way
through, switch off the oven when cooked and leave them in overnight to dry out. Serve on
their own or with whipped cream and seasonal berries.

'Chocolate cream meringues . . . . still warm and treacly inside their chocolate envelopes.'

TARTE AU CITRON (WITH A CHOCOLATE TWIST)

A little chocolate goes a long way in this variation on one of my favourite recipes. A perfectly balanced combination of sour lemon and bittersweet chocolate, just ready to melt on the tongue.

Takes 1½ hours / serves 6–8

Pastry
150g plain flour
75g butter, cold and cubed
25g unrefined caster sugar
1 egg

Filling 1
2 eggs
50g unrefined caster sugar
zest and juice of 2 unwaxed lemons
175ml double cream

Filling 2
60g dark chocolate, broken into small, even-sized pieces
100ml double cream

Place the flour and butter in a bowl and rub together until it resembles breadcrumbs. Add the sugar and mix through. Beat the egg, and mix it through the dry ingredients with a knife, until the pastry comes together in a dough ball. Then wrap in cling film and chill for 30 minutes.

Heat the oven to 190°C/gas mark 5. Butter a 23cm loose-bottomed flan case.

Roll the pastry out on a lightly dusted, cool surface to fit the flan case. (Do not stretch the pastry to fit or it will shrink while cooking.) Trim away the excess pastry from the edges. Prick the base with a fork, line with baking parchment, fill with baking beans and bake for 20 minutes. Reduce the oven to 150°C/gas mark 2, take the pastry case from the oven, remove the beans and parchment, and return to the oven and cook for a further 10 minutes.

Meanwhile, make filling 1 by whisking together the eggs, sugar, lemon juice, zest and cream. To make filling 2, melt the chocolate in a bain-marie, then add the cream and stir until smooth.

Now assemble your work of art. Pour all the lemon mixture into the pastry case, then slowly pour in the chocolate in thin circular drizzles. Using a slim knife, swirl the mixture a little to create a marbled look. Place in the middle of the hot oven (150°C/gas mark 2) for 30 minutes until just set, and serve hot or cold.

ROUX'S GINGER CRUMBLE

This golden-topped crumble combines stem ginger with autumn fruit and just a little chocolate. Spicy, yet mellow. Just like Roux.

Takes 1 hour / serves 6

Crumble topping
butter for greasing dish
200g plain flour
100g unrefined caster sugar
120g butter

Filling
100g unrefined caster sugar
100ml hot water
75g stem ginger, chopped
3 cooking apples
3 pears
100g chocolate, grated

Heat the oven to 200°C/gas mark 6. Butter a large ovenproof dish.

Rub together the flour, caster sugar and butter until it resembles breadcrumbs.

To make the filling, dissolve the sugar in the water and add the chopped ginger to the syrup. Peel and core the apples and pears, chop into even-sized chunks and place in the baking dish. Pour the ginger syrup over the fruit. Top with the grated chocolate, then with the crumble mix and an extra sprinkling of sugar.

Place in the middle of the oven and cook for 20 minutes. Reduce the oven to 160°C/gas mark 2 and cook for a further 15 minutes until golden and bubbling.

Madame du Barry, mistress of Louis XV of France, used to encourage her many lovers to take chocolate to maintain their sexual prowess.

MARBLED MENDIANTS

These traditional chocolates – thus named after the beggars who sold them door-to-door – are irresistibly pretty and really very easy to make. I used to make them with my daughter Anouchka when she was only four years old – I find that children generally love arranging the pieces of fruit on the top – and even now, they're among my favourites.

Takes 1 hour / makes 50

300g dark or milk chocolate, broken
  into small, even-sized pieces
200g white chocolate, broken into
  small, even-sized pieces
150g mixture of almonds, walnuts,
  raisins, sultanas, pistachio nuts or
  candied fruit

Place the dark chocolate in a bain-marie and melt. Bring the temperature of the chocolate to 55°C, then remove from the bain-marie and cool back to a temperature of 27–28°C, mixing constantly. Return to its bain-marie and bring back to a temperature of 31–32°C. If using milk chocolate, follow the instructions on page 16.

Place the white chocolate in a bain-marie and melt. Bring the temperature of the chocolate to 50°C, then remove from the bain-marie and cool back to a temperature of 26–27°C, mixing constantly. Return to its bain-marie and bring back to a temperature of 29–30°C.

On a sheet of baking parchment or marble, spoon out $^2/_3$ teaspoon of the dark chocolate and $^1/_3$ white chocolate on top, and using the back of a teaspoon quickly shape into a round disc 2.5cm in diameter. Sprinkle on a few nuts or pieces of dried fruit and leave to cool and set.

CÉLESTE PRALINE CHEESECAKE

The term 'praline' has existed since the sixteenth century, and was originally a whole almond coated in hard sugar. Nowadays the term is a general one, referring to any confection made from sugar, nuts and chocolate. For this luscious cheesecake I'm using a favourite combination of hazelnuts, cream and dark chocolate.

Takes 3½ hours / serves 8

Base
150g digestive biscuits
100g ground hazelnuts
100g butter

Topping
200g dark chocolate, broken into
   small, even-sized pieces
125ml double cream
250g cream cheese
75g unrefined caster sugar
100g hazelnuts

Place the digestive biscuits in a blender and whizz to a fine crumb. Mix in the ground hazelnuts. Melt the butter and mix it into the biscuit crumb and hazelnut mixture. Tip into a 20cm loose-bottomed round tin, spread evenly and press down with the back of a spoon.

For the topping, melt the chocolate in a bain-marie. Add the cream and blend until smooth. Whisk the cream cheese to soften, add the chocolate mixture and sugar, and blend. Pour into the prepared tin, smooth over the top and scatter with the hazelnuts. Place in the fridge to set for 3 hours, then carefully run a thin bladed knife around the edge to help release the cheesecake and remove from the tin.

Some seventeenth-century clerics associated chocolate with heretical and impious behaviour, calling it 'the damnable agent of necromancers and sorcerers'.

GRIMMS' CHERRY CAKE

The Black Forest is the source of many of the Grimms' dark fairy tales – where Little Red Riding Hood first encountered the wolf; where Hansel and Gretel found the gingerbread house; and, if we believe the stories, where the idea first came from to combine dark chocolate and black cherries to make one of the world's favourite flavours. In this version, the sour-sweet tang of fresh cherries gives this unctuous cake a deceptively summery freshness . . .

Takes 1½ hours, plus cooling / serves 8–12

butter for greasing tins
10 eggs, separated
200g unrefined caster sugar
100g cocoa powder

Topping
150g dark chocolate, broken into
  small, even-sized pieces
100g fresh cherries, stalks left on
150ml double cream

Filling
425g tin stoned morello cherries
3 tbsp kirsch, or cherry juice
300ml double cream
150g mascarpone
125g morello cherry jam

Heat the oven to 180°C/gas mark 4. Butter and line three 20cm-diameter loose-bottomed non-stick cake tins. Put the egg yolks into a mixing bowl, then add the sugar. Whisk rapidly until stiff. Sift in the cocoa and quickly fold in with a metal spoon until evenly blended.

Whisk the egg whites until they form stiff peaks. Quickly fold the two mixtures together and divide evenly between the tins. Bake in the middle of the oven for 20 minutes. Cool for 10 minutes, then turn out on to a cooling wire, peel off the parchment and leave until totally cold.

To make the topping, melt the chocolate in a bain-marie. Dip the fresh cherries into the chocolate, then place them on baking parchment. Heat the 150ml double cream, then add to the melted chocolate and mix well. To make the filling, drain the morello cherries, reserving the juice; add the kirsch to the juice. Whisk the 300ml double cream until softly whipped, add the mascarpone and mix until evenly blended.

Spoon 3 tablespoons of the kirsch mixture over one of the cakes. Spread with half the cherry jam, top with half the whipped cream and scatter with half the drained cherries. Lay the second cake on top and repeat, then put the last sponge in place and spoon the remaining kirsch mixture over it. Spread the chocolate cream over the top and decorate with the chocolate-dipped cherries.

AZTEC CHOCOLATE ORANGE CAKE

**This light but decadent chocolate-orange cake also looks marvellous
sprinkled with a little edible gold leaf . . .**

Takes 50 minutes, plus cooling / serves 8

butter for greasing tin
200g butter, soft
200g unrefined golden
  caster sugar
4 eggs, beaten
zest of 2 unwaxed oranges
200g self-raising flour
juice of 1 orange

Syrup
juice of 2 oranges
75g unrefined golden
  caster sugar

Topping
100ml double cream
150g dark chocolate, broken into
  small, even-sized pieces
zest of 1 unwaxed orange
edible gold leaf (optional)

Heat the oven to 180°C/gas mark 4. Butter a 24cm non-stick savarin cake tin.

Place the butter and sugar in a bowl and beat together until soft and creamy. Add the eggs and
orange zest and whisk until blended. Add the flour and fold in quickly. Then add the orange
juice and transfer to the prepared savarin tin. Cook in the middle of the oven for 30 minutes
until the cake is well risen and a knife inserted in the centre comes out clean.

To make the syrup, place the orange juice and sugar in a small pan on a gentle heat and mix
until all the sugar has dissolved. Remove from the heat and cool.

Remove the cake from the oven and spoon the orange syrup over it. Leave to sit for 5 minutes,
then turn the cake out on to a cooling wire.

To make the topping, heat the cream in a small pan. Melt the chocolate in a bain-marie, add
the cream and blend until smooth. Leave to cool until the mixture thickens enough to coat the
back of a spoon. Place a tray under the cooling rack and spoon the chocolate coating over the
cake evenly. Finally, top with orange zest (or some edible gold leaf) and leave to set.

PISTACHIO AND CHOCOLATE SHORTBREAD

Pistachio and chocolate is an unusual, but delicious, combination. Serve on its own, or with pistachio ice cream . . .

Takes 45 minutes / makes approx. 20

120g pistachios, peeled
150g butter, soft
75g unrefined caster sugar
200g plain flour
20g cocoa powder
1 egg yolk
icing sugar

Heat the oven to 180°C/gas mark 4. Line a baking sheet with baking parchment.

Place the pistachio nuts in a food processor and whizz until finely ground. Add the butter, sugar, flour and cocoa powder and blend until mixed evenly, then add the egg yolk and mix to form a dough ball.

Lightly dust a surface with sifted icing sugar and roll the dough out to approximately 1–2cm thick. Using a 9cm pastry-cutter, press out discs and place on the baking sheet. Gather up all the excess dough and knead together, roll out and repeat until all the dough is used.

Place in the middle of the oven and cook for 10 minutes. Remove from the oven and leave to cool and set on the baking sheet for 10 minutes before transferring to a cooling wire.

'I know everyone's favourites. Trust me, this is yours.'

CLASSIC FRENCH MACARONS

Macarons (or 'macaroons') is a term taken from the Italian *maccarone*. Unlike the English macaroon, which is most often based on coconut, these are traditionally a meringue base of eggs, icing sugar, ground almonds and a variety of flavours, most often sandwiched together with ganache or a fruit-based filling. These are a little less easy to make than the smaller ones on page 92 – but it's worth the practice. Fran likes a ganache filling for these, although I like to cut the richness of the chocolate with a berry-fruit jam instead – sour cherry or blackcurrant both work very well.

Takes 1 hour, plus cooling / makes approx. 20 sandwiched macaroons

4 large egg whites
200g unrefined caster sugar
115g icing sugar
30g ground almonds
4g cocoa powder

Filling
50g dark chocolate, broken into
small, even-sized pieces
2 tbsp double cream

Heat the oven to 150°C/gas mark 3. Line two large baking sheets with baking parchment.

Beat the egg whites until standing in peaks. Add the sugar, and whisk until stiff and shiny. In a food processor, whizz the icing sugar, ground almonds and cocoa until really fine, then sift into a bowl. Don't try to skip this stage; discard any lumps that will not pass through the sieve. Add to the egg whites, folding in with a spatula, and mix until evenly blended. Do not over mix.

Put the mixture into a piping bag and pipe on to the baking parchment in 4.5cm blobs. Bang the baking trays firmly on the work surface four times to remove the air. Leave to stand for 5 minutes.

Place in the middle of the oven and cook for 15 minutes. Transfer to the bottom of the oven for a further 10–15 minutes. Remove from the oven, slip the baking parchment with the macaroons off the baking sheet and leave to cool.

For the filling, place the chocolate in a bain-marie along with the cream and melt. Remove from the bain-marie, mix and cool until it is stiff. Spread a little on one macaroon half, place another half to the filling and gently sandwich together.

MARIANNE'S CHOCOLATE PUDDING

This rich, double chocolate pudding is named after my editor, a true chocoholic, who can always be relied upon to choose the most indulgent chocolate desserts (while I tend to opt for the cheese board!).

Takes 1 hour / serves 6–8

butter for greasing dish
75g unrefined caster sugar
40g butter, soft
1 egg
40g cocoa powder
150g self-raising flour
120ml milk

Sauce
180g unrefined soft brown sugar
200ml water
40g cocoa powder
1 tsp vanilla extract

Heat oven to 180°C/gas mark 4. Rub the inside of a 1-litre ovenproof dish with a little butter.

In a bowl, place the sugar, butter and egg and whisk until blended. Add the cocoa powder and flour along with a little milk and blend until smooth. Add the remaining milk and mix in, then transfer to the buttered baking dish.

To make the sauce, place the sugar, water and cocoa in a small saucepan. Heat gently and mix until dissolved. Add the vanilla extract, pour over the top of the cake mixture, place in the middle of the oven and cook for 30 minutes. Serve with vanilla ice cream.

When Columbus returned to Spain in 1502 from his fourth voyage to the New World, he introduced a new drink to the Spanish court. King Ferdinand and Queen Isabel were not impressed, however, dismissing the chocolate as a bizarre tribal concoction.

OMI'S COCONUT PEACHES

Readers of *Peaches for Monsieur le Curé* will no doubt remember Omi, the playful, elderly Muslim lady who declared herself 'too old for Ramadan'. I'd always wondered exactly how she prepared the peaches from Armande's tree. Given Omi's love of coconut and Armande's love of chocolate, I think this just may be it.

Takes 20 minutes / serves 4

4 ripe peaches
100g dark chocolate, broken into
  small, even-sized pieces
1 tbsp desiccated coconut

Cut the peaches in half, then into quarters and remove the stone. Melt the chocolate in a bain-marie. Dip one side of each of the peach wedges into the chocolate and then the desiccated coconut, place on baking parchment and leave to set. Serve on their own, or with ice cream.

The Spanish guarded the secret of chocolate for almost 100 years, during which time they planted cocoa in their overseas colonies, setting the scene for what was to become a global commodity.

CHILLI-CHOCOLATE SHOTS

**I like these rich, spiced chocolate shots as heavy on the chilli as possible –
the combination of flavours is heady, strong and invigorating. Add a touch
of Aztec gold by decorating with edible gold leaf . . .**

Takes 2½ hours / serves 6

400ml double cream
*½ tsp chopped medium-hot
  red chilli (more, if you're
  feeling heroic)*
*250g dark chocolate, broken
  into small, even-sized pieces*
cocoa powder, for dusting
6 small slices of chilli
edible gold leaf (optional)

Gently warm the cream in a small saucepan, add the chopped chilli and chocolate, then stir
until all the chocolate has dissolved and is blended. It will form a rich, luscious mixture.

Divide into six small pots (I use demitasse coffee cups and shiny glasses). Top with a dusting of
cocoa and a little slice of chilli. Cool in the fridge for a couple of hours.

*The Aztecs associated chocolate with Xochiquetzal, goddess of fertility,
believing that cacao seeds originated in Paradise and would bless
consumers with spiritual wisdom, energy and sexual powers.*

ROULADE BICOLORE

The word 'roulade' is from the French, meaning 'to roll', and this cake
has both sweet and savoury relatives all over Europe. This stylish-looking
chocolate roulade is related to the traditional Bûche de Noël – or chocolate
log – but it's too good to keep for Christmas. Just leave off the plastic robin
and enjoy it anytime . . .

Takes 2 hours / serves 8

150g dark chocolate, broken into
  small, even-sized pieces
6 eggs, separated
170g unrefined caster sugar
20g cocoa powder

Topping
300ml double cream
1 tbsp icing sugar

Heat the oven to 180°C/gas mark 4. Carefully line the base and sides of a 31 x 21cm roulade
tin with baking parchment.

Place the chocolate in a bain-marie and melt. Whisk the egg whites with an electric whisk
until stiff. In another bowl, whisk the egg yolks and sugar until thick and creamy, then add
the melted chocolate and blend. Pour this mixture into the whisked egg whites, along with the
cocoa powder. Whisk until evenly blended.

Pour the mixture into the prepared baking tin. Smooth over the top, place in the middle of
the oven and cook for 25 minutes. Remove, leave to cool in the tin for 10 minutes, then place
a large sheet of baking parchment and a tray on top and invert. Lift off the tin, peel away the
baking parchment and leave to cool completely.

For the topping, whip the cream until it stands in soft peaks, then spread over the roulade,
leaving a small cream-free margin around the edge. Make a knife cut 8cm along the 31cm
long side, cutting just halfway through the roulade (this helps to get a tighter roll). Now tightly
roll long side to long side, using the sheet of parchment to help keep it tight. Twist each end
of the parchment tightly – this helps to improve the shape. Place in the fridge for 30 minutes,
then unwrap by peeling away the parchment carefully, retaining the log shape. Transfer on to
a serving board, placing the join underneath, and dust with icing sugar or cocoa.

PETITS INNOCENTS PUDDINGS

These innocent-looking little white chocolate puddings conceal a dark and secret heart. Serve with whipped cream or ice cream for maximum angelic effect.

Takes 2 hours / serves 6

Filling (for freezing)
50g dark chocolate, broken into
  small, even-sized pieces
100ml double cream

Puddings
80g white chocolate, broken into
  small, even-sized pieces
150g butter, soft
150g unrefined caster sugar
3 eggs

3 tbsp milk
½ tsp vanilla extract
200g self-raising flour
200ml whipped cream,
  for serving

First make the filling by gently heating the chocolate in a bain-marie until melted. Add the cream and stir until blended. Line six compartments of an ice-cube tray with cling film, then divide the chocolate sauce between them and place in the freezer for 1 hour or until solid.

Heat the oven to 180°C/gas mark 4. Butter six 8.5cm pudding moulds or ramekins generously.

Place the white chocolate in a bain-marie and heat gently until melted, then remove from the heat. Chop the butter and place in a mixing bowl along with the sugar and whisk until creamy and soft. Add the eggs, whisk, then pour in the melted chocolate, milk and vanilla extract, and whisk again. Add the flour and fold in quickly.

Three-quarters-fill the prepared pudding moulds, then remove the frozen dark-chocolate cubes from the ice tray and insert one cube into the middle of each pudding. Top with more sponge mixture, spreading it over to seal in each frozen cube. Place in the middle of the oven and cook for 25 minutes. Carefully turn out each little pudding and serve with a dollop of whipped cream or ice cream.

'A promise, half-fulfilled, of the forbidden . . .'

JOE'S 'SPECIALS' TRIFLE

Readers of *Blackberry Wine* will remember Joe Cox, the ex-miner, gardener and sometime magician, based on my English grandfather. From my knowledge of both of them, I think they would appreciate this English recipe with a twist – rhubarb goes surprisingly well with chocolate, providing a nice, tart contrast. My grandfather – an enthusiastic grower of many species of rhubarb – would almost certainly have substituted a splash of his own rhubarb wine for the Vin Santo, but for those who don't have access to that extraordinary vintage, Vin Santo will do nicely.

Takes 2 hours / serves 8

Custard	Filling	Topping
2 tbsp custard powder	500g rhubarb	200ml double cream
400ml milk	50g unrefined caster sugar	200ml mascarpone
2 tbsp sugar	250g Italian biscotti	20g white chocolate, grated
2 tbsp cocoa powder	100ml Vin Santo, or other liqueur	20g dark chocolate, grated
		25g flaked almonds, toasted

First make the custard. Dissolve the custard powder in a little of the milk. Heat the rest of the milk, then, when almost boiling, pour on to the dissolved custard powder and stir. Add the sugar and cocoa and return to the pan, stirring on a low heat until it thickens. Remove from the heat and place a layer of cling film directly on to the custard. (This will stop a skin from forming.) Leave to cool.

Chop the rhubarb into 5cm lengths and place in a saucepan with 2 tablespoons water and the caster sugar. Heat gently with a lid on for 4 minutes, then remove from the heat and leave to cool.

Place the biscotti in a large glass bowl or individual glasses, add the Vin Santo, top with the prepared fruit, then spoon the cooled chocolate custard over. Whisk the cream until it stands in very soft peaks, add the mascarpone and blend until smooth. Spoon the cream mixture over the custard, and finally top with the grated chocolate and toasted almonds.

RASPBERRY MARQUISE

This is the ultimate chocoholic's dessert. Grown-up, rich and seductive, it's best served with a fresh raspberry coulis to cut the richness of the chocolate. Perfect for dinner parties, a little goes a long way – and because it's flourless, it's the ideal chocolate fix for cacao addicts everywhere.

Takes 20 minutes, plus 2 hours (minimum) to set / serves 10–12

175g butter
175g unrefined caster sugar
400g dark chocolate, broken into
  small, even-sized pieces
40g cocoa powder

500ml double cream
6 egg yolks, beaten
cocoa powder, for dusting
250g raspberries

Carefully line a 11.5 x 25.5cm tin with cling film (try to avoid creases).

Place the butter, sugar, chocolate and cocoa in a bain-marie, melt and stir until smooth and blended. Whisk the cream in a bowl until it just starts to hold, add the egg yolks, whisk, then add the chocolate mixture and blend until smooth. Pour into the lined tin, bang twice on the work surface to remove any air pockets from the corners and place in the fridge for 2 hours or overnight until set.

Turn the loaf out on to a flat board or plate, peel away the cling film and lightly dust with sifted cocoa. Blend half the raspberries and sieve to remove the seeds. (Fran suggests doing this, but I never bother. I guess it depends on whether you care about raspberry seeds.) Just before serving, arrange the remaining raspberries on top of the loaf, drizzle with the coulis and serve. Have a jug of hot water to dip the knife into before each slice; this will help to achieve a neat cut.

Napoleon always carried chocolate with him, which
he ate whenever he needed an energy boost.

SACHERTORTE

This rich and spectacular torte was originally created in 1832 for Prince Wenzel von Metternich by Franz Sacher, a sixteen-year-old apprentice chef who happened to be in charge one night after the head chef was taken ill. Since then, it has become one of the best-known chocolate desserts in the world – and it's still so simple that a sixteen-year-old could make it!

Takes 50 minutes, plus cooling / serves 6–8

butter for greasing tin
200g dark chocolate, broken into
small, even-sized pieces
5 eggs
250g unrefined caster sugar
2 tsp coffee
150g ground almonds

Icing
150g dark chocolate, broken into
small, even-sized pieces
50g butter
1 tbsp golden syrup

Heat the oven to 180°C/gas mark 4. Grease a 20cm non-stick loose-bottomed non-stick cake tin.

Melt the chocolate in a bain-marie. Separate the eggs; whisk the yolks and sugar with an electric whisk, until thick and creamy. Whisk the egg whites until they stand in stiff peaks. Dissolve the coffee in 2 tablespoons of hot water. Add the ground almonds, dissolved coffee and melted chocolate to the egg yolks. Mix well. Add the egg whites and fold in until smooth and blended.

Pour into the prepared cake tin and bake for 30 minutes in the middle of the oven, then cover with foil and cook for a further 10 minutes. To check if the cake is cooked insert a knife in the centre; it should come out clean. If it doesn't, return the cake to the oven for 5 more minutes. When cooked, remove from the oven and leave to cool in the tin for 5 minutes. Release the base from the cake tin, allow the cake to cool totally on the bottom, then carefully remove using a palette knife and sit the cake on a cooling wire.

To make the icing, melt the chocolate, butter and golden syrup on a very low heat, stirring occasionally, until smooth and glossy. Place the cooling wire over a tray, then pour the icing over the cake and, with the back of a metal spoon, carefully work and spread the chocolate icing all over, taking care on the sides. Leave to set for at least 1 hour, then transfer to a flat serving plate.

'BRIOCHE JULIETTE'

'Juliette Brioche' was the nickname given to Juliette Binoche by my six-year-old daughter when Juliette first came to stay at our house before filming *Chocolat*. She has a very lively sense of humour, and I think she'd enjoy the idea of having a chocolate cake named after her.

Takes 1 hour, plus 2 hours' or more proving / makes 1 loaf

butter for greasing tin
200g just-warm milk
7g dried yeast
50g unrefined caster sugar
500g strong white flour
1 tsp salt

125g butter, soft
2 eggs, beaten
150g plain chocolate, roughly
   chopped into small pieces
egg, for glazing

Butter the inside of a 1kg loaf tin.

Mix together the warm milk, yeast and sugar and leave to sit for 5 minutes.

Using a mixer with a dough hook, place the flour, salt and butter in a bowl and blend until the mixture resembles breadcrumbs. Add the yeast liquid and the egg, then beat on a slow speed for 5 minutes until the mixture is even and smoothly blended.

On a floured surface work the dough into a rectangle approximately 30 x 38cm. Scatter the chocolate pieces evenly over the dough, then roll the dough like a Swiss roll and gently pat into shape to fit the loaf tin. Place in the buttered tin and leave to rise until it has doubled in size. This can take 2 hours on a warm day or overnight in the winter!

Heat the oven to 200°C/gas mark 6.

Brush the top of the brioche with beaten egg, place in the middle of the oven and cook for 35 minutes. Best eaten while still warm.

JOSÉPHINE'S FLOURLESS CHOCOLATE CAKE

This flourless chocolate cake is rich, dark and guaranteed to deliver just the right kind of punch. I like it the way it is, straight out of the oven, but the crème fraîche and raspberry topping give it a grown-up, elegant balance of flavours.

Takes 2 hours / serves 8

butter for greasing tin
300g dark chocolate, broken into
  small, even-sized pieces
200g butter
6 eggs, separated
200g unrefined caster sugar
1 tsp vanilla extract

Topping
200ml crème fraîche
225g fresh raspberries

Heat the oven to 180°C/gas mark 4. Butter a 20cm loose-bottomed non-stick cake tin and line with baking parchment.

Melt the chocolate and butter in a bain-marie. Whisk the egg whites until they are firm and stand in peaks, and then, in a separate bowl, whisk the yolks and sugar until light and creamy. Add the melted chocolate and vanilla extract and blend. Add this to the egg whites and whisk until evenly mixed.

Pour into the prepared cake tin and place in the middle of the oven for 45 minutes. Remove from the oven, cool for 5 minutes, then carefully remove the cake from the tin. (The cake may collapse and crack at this stage, but this is normal – and besides, you're going to top it with raspberries and cream.) Leave to cool completely, then casually spread the top with crème fraîche and finish with a cluster of fresh raspberries.

POACHED PEARS IN CHOCOLATE, WITH MULLED-WINE JELLY

Three of my favourite things in one: this autumnal classic combines red wine, chocolate and ripe pears to make a spicy, fresh dessert. Perfect for those still-mellow autumn evenings . . .

Takes 4 hours / serves 6

1 bottle red wine
200g unrefined caster sugar
1 cinnamon stick
1 star anise
6 pears
7g gelatine

Dipping sauce
150g chocolate, broken into
 small, even-sized pieces
1 tbsp golden syrup
icing sugar, for dusting

Place the red wine, sugar, cinnamon stick and star anise in a saucepan and gently bring to a simmer. Carefully peel the pears, leaving on the stalks. Place the pears in the wine, trying to submerge them completely; if you can't, keep turning them to marinate. Place a lid on the saucepan, bring to the boil and simmer for 10 minutes. Remove from the heat, leaving the pears in the pan to steep for 1 hour. Remove the pears and place on a cooling wire for 2 hours so that they dry off on the outside.

Measure off 250ml of the marinating wine and dissolve 7g of granulated or sheet gelatine into the liquid. Pour into an approximately 10 x 10cm square container, place in the fridge and leave to set for 2 hours.

To make the sauce, melt the chocolate and golden syrup in a bain-marie and mix until smooth. Carefully spoon the chocolate sauce over each pear, place them on a baking sheet and leave to set in a cool place.

Dip the set wine container in hot water for 30 seconds, turn out the jelly on to a chopping board and cut into 6 cubes or little love hearts. Place the chocolate-dipped pears on serving plates, dust with a little icing sugar and add 1 wine-jelly cube to each.

CONQUISTADOR ORANGE PUDDING

Chocolate and orange has long been considered one of the classic combinations. This wonderful pudding contains a whole fresh orange at its heart, which infuses the cooking with its bittersweet flavour. Sanguinello oranges work well in this recipe (what we used to call 'blood oranges' when we were children), to add a little extra bite.

Takes 2½ hours / serves 6–8

butter for greasing tin	150g unrefined caster sugar
1 whole unwaxed orange	3 eggs
100g dark chocolate, broken into small, even-sized pieces	25g cocoa powder
	150g self-raising flour
150g butter	2 tbsp milk

Butter a 1kg pudding basin (be generous). Cut into the orange skin and flesh six times, approximately 2cm in depth; this will allow the flavours to infuse the pudding.

In a bain-marie, melt the chocolate. Using an electric whisk, blend together the butter and sugar, add the eggs and whisk again. Pour in the melted chocolate, add the cocoa and whisk until smooth. Fold in the flour until blended, then mix in the milk.

Spoon one third of the mixture into the prepared pudding basin, place the orange in the middle, then add the remaining mixture and spread to seal in the orange. Cover with cling film and tie with string, making a handle to lift. Put in a large saucepan, pour in enough hot water to come halfway up the side of the pudding basin, then place on the hob with a lid on and bring to the boil. Reduce to a gentle simmer for 2 hours, constantly checking the water and adding more if needed. Carefully remove from the saucepan, gently ease a palette knife around the edge, place a large plate on top, invert and give it a shake and lift the pudding basin off. Serve with chocolate sauce or ice cream.

When Cortez's conquistadors plundered Emperor Montezuma's palace they found not silver and gold but huge quantities of cacao beans.

CHOCOLATE NOUGAT

I've always loved nougat in all its forms. This chocolate version works well with almonds or pistachios, but also with dried cherries or apricots.

Takes 1 hour / serves 12

rice paper
450g unrefined caster sugar
150g liquid glucose
  (available at chemists)
150ml water

2 egg whites
20g cocoa powder
350g pistachios, almonds,
  or dried fruit

Line an 18cm shallow round tin or small pudding bowl with rice paper.

Place the sugar, liquid glucose and water in a pan and gently bring to the boil. Reduce to a simmer and continue to cook until the temperature reaches 140°C (use a sugar thermometer to check). This will take about 8–10 minutes.

Whisk the egg whites until stiff and standing in white peaks. Still whisking continually, pour in half the sugar syrup little by little – the mixture will thicken. Add the cocoa powder and nuts or dried fruit and continue to whisk. Return the remaining syrup to the heat and bring back to a simmer. When it is liquid again, slowly pour it into the egg white mixture and whisk for a further few minutes. The mixture will then have taken on a thick, sticky consistency.

Transfer to the rice-paper-lined container and, with a metal spoon dipped in hot water, smooth down the top of the nougat. Dust with a little extra cocoa powder and leave to cool and set overnight. Cut into wedges with a hot knife.

The English were slow to understand the value of the cacao bean. On at least two occasions, when English pirates took Spanish ships loaded with beans, they dumped the priceless cargo.

GAUFRES AU CHOCOLAT

The word 'waffle' derives from the Dutch, and dates back to the Middle Ages, while the waffle iron, also very old, seems to be a direct descendant of the irons designed to make Communion wafers. Waffles of all kinds have been a popular street food throughout continental Europe since the thirteenth century and are still sold, dusted with sugar or with whipped cream, from kiosks throughout France and Belgium. This recipe for chocolate waffles is great on its own with a sifting of sugar; even better with a seductive marriage of mixed berries and whipped cream. (Fran doesn't add anything to the whipped cream, but for my version of crème Chantilly, try adding a teaspoonful of icing sugar and a splash of kirsch to the cream as you whip it. Trust me: it makes a difference.)

Takes 15 minutes / makes 8 waffles

300g self-raising flour
½ tsp baking powder
20g unrefined caster sugar
400ml milk
90ml vegetable oil

2 eggs
20g cocoa powder
1 tbsp icing sugar
500g mixed berries
200ml double cream, whipped

Place the flour, baking powder, caster sugar, milk, vegetable oil, eggs and cocoa in a bowl and mix until smooth and blended. Leave to sit for 10 minutes.

Heat the waffle-maker, lightly oil the plates and fill each with approximately 90ml of the batter (sizes of waffle makers do vary so you may need slightly more or less). Close the lid and cook for 2 minutes. Remove and repeat until all the mixture is used.

Dust with icing sugar and serve with berries and whipped cream.

CHOCOLATE AND HAZELNUT SPREAD

Ever since my trip to the Nutella factory I've wondered how easy it would be to try to create my own chocolate spread. Turns out it's surprisingly easy – the result isn't Nutella, but (dare I say it) it's just as delicious. All you need is a spoon . . .

Takes 1 hour / makes 2 x 250g jars

150g hazelnuts, toasted and peeled
75g icing sugar
250g dark or milk chocolate, broken
  into small, even-sized pieces
25g butter
100ml double cream
a pinch of salt

Place the hazelnuts in a food processor and whizz until smooth. Add the icing sugar and blend. Warm the chocolate, butter and cream in a bain-marie until smooth and melted, add to the whizzed nuts and icing sugar in the food processor along with a pinch of salt and blend until smooth.

Place two clean glass jars, with their lids beside them, on a baking sheet and put them in the oven at 140 °C/gas mark 1 for 20 minutes to sterilize. The jars can also be sterilized in a hot wash in the dishwasher.

Transfer the chocolate spread to the jars and leave to cool and set. It is best used at room temperature to ease spreading, but needs to be stored in the fridge.

Chocolate manufacturers currently use 40% of the world's almonds and 20% of the world's peanuts.

'Everyone needs a little luxury, a little self-indulgence from time to time.'

REYNAUD'S BLACK-AND-WHITE LAYER CAKE

Purists believe that white chocolate doesn't officially count as chocolate at all. This means that you can enjoy this dramatic-looking layer cake with only half the guilt . . .

Takes 1 hour 10 minutes, plus cooling / serves 8–12

Ganache
500ml double cream
500g white chocolate, broken into small, even-sized pieces

Cake
butter, for greasing
190g self-raising flour
40g cocoa powder
200g butter, soft and cut into small cubes

200g golden syrup
1 tsp baking powder
4 eggs, beaten
125g dark chocolate, broken into small, even-sized pieces
50ml shot of strong espresso

To make the ganache, heat the cream in a saucepan until just simmering. Then remove from the heat and add the white chocolate. Stir until melted and smooth. Leave to cool and thicken (this will take at least an hour – you *can* put it in the fridge, but check and stir it regularly so that it doesn't set too hard). It needs a spreadable consistency, like heavy whipped cream.

Heat the oven to 180°C/gas mark 4. Butter two 20cm non-stick cake tins and line the bases with baking parchment.

In a mixing bowl, place the flour, cocoa, butter, golden syrup, baking powder and eggs, then beat quickly with an electric mixer until creamy and blended. Melt the dark chocolate in a bain-marie, then pour it and the espresso shot into the mixture and blend until even. Divide the mixture between the two cake tins, place in the middle of the oven and bake for 25 minutes, until a knife inserted into the centres comes out clean. Cool in the tins for 5 minutes, then turn the cakes out on to a cooling wire, peel away the parchment and leave until cold.

Slice each cake in half horizontally, making four layers in total. Spread a small spoonful of the ganache in the middle of a serving plate. Stick a layer of cake on top. Spread with a layer of ganache, top with another cake and repeat until all four layers are used. Finally, top the cake and sides with a good layer of ganache. Leave to set for at least 30 minutes in a cool place.

YIN-YANG CHOCOLATE SAUCE

This is really two recipes in one – and of course you could use either the dark or the white chocolate sauce on its own – but there's something enticing about the combination of flavours. One balances the other – like the yin-yang principle – and so when you're eating it (with ice cream, cake, crushed amaretti, autumn fruit or just on its own, with a spoon) you can be sure that the universe approves as much as you do.

Takes 10 minutes / serves 6–8

Dark
100g dark chocolate, broken into
  small, even-sized pieces
100ml double cream

White
100g white chocolate, broken into
  small, even-sized pieces
100ml double cream

You'll need two bain-maries for this – one for the dark chocolate, the other for the white. In each bain-marie, gently melt the chocolate and cream, mixing until you have two smooth and blended chocolate sauces. Pour both into the same jug and use a knife to stir the mixture to create a marbled look. (Don't over-mix – you want to keep the black-and-white effect.)

Serve over ice cream, cake, amaretti, fruit or chocolate brownies.

Chocolate as we know it was developed in 1847 by J.S. Fry & Sons, who produced the first solid chocolate bar by mixing sugar with cocoa powder and cocoa butter. The Cadburys brothers followed soon after.

RIVER-GYPSY BANANA BREAD

There's a wholesome, nostalgic nuttiness to this wholemeal banana-chocolate loaf that makes it the perfect complement to a cup of indulgent hot chocolate . . .

Takes 1 hour / serves 8

butter for greasing tin
200g self-raising wholemeal flour
1 tsp baking powder
100g unrefined brown sugar
100g milk chocolate, broken into
  small, even-sized pieces

2 eggs
100ml vegetable oil
3 ripe bananas, mashed

Heat the oven to 180°C/gas mark 4. Butter a 1kg loaf tin and line it with baking parchment.

Place the flour, baking powder, sugar and chocolate in a mixing bowl. Mix well. In a jug, place the eggs, oil and bananas and whizz with a hand-held blender until smooth. Then pour into the flour mix and blend quickly until stiff.

Put the mixture into the prepared loaf tin, sprinkle the top of the cake with some extra brown sugar, place in the middle of the oven and bake for 45 minutes. Test for readiness by inserting a knife into the middle of the cake: the blade should come out clean when it's ready. Turn out the cake on to a cooling wire and cool. Eat warm or cold.

MACARONS ST-FRANCIS

I love these tubby little macaroons, which, when they're finished, look just like well-fed little Franciscan friars . . .

Takes 1 hour / makes approx. 15 sandwiched macaroons

Macaroons	Filling
150g unrefined soft light brown sugar	*50g dark chocolate, broken into small, even-sized pieces*
250g ground almonds	*2 tbsp double cream*
12g cocoa powder	
2 egg whites	
½ tsp vanilla extract	

Heat the oven to 180°C/gas mark 4. Line a baking sheet with baking parchment.

Place the sugar and almonds in a food processor and whizz until smooth. Add the cocoa, egg whites and vanilla extract, then whizz again until blended. The mixture will be stiff, but place it in a piping bag and pipe out little blobs approximately 4cm across on to the baking parchment.

Place in the middle of the oven and bake for 20–25 minutes. When cooked, lift the parchment with the macaroons from the baking sheet so that the macaroons do not continue cooking. Leave to cool, then peel off the parchment.

To make the filling, place the chocolate and cream together in a bain-marie and melt. Remove the bowl from the bain-marie, mix and cool until the mixture is stiff, then spread a little on one macaroon half, place another half on the filling and gently sandwich together.

At first, the Catholic Church mistrusted chocolate. Clerics were bitterly divided on whether it counted as a drink rather than a food, in which case it could be taken on fast days.

CHILLI CHOCOLATE INGOTS

The mixture of chilli flakes and sea salt on these irregular chocolate chunks is intense and evocative . . .

Takes 30 minutes, plus cooling / serves 6

350g dark chocolate, broken into
  small, even-sized pieces
½ tsp chilli flakes
½ tsp sea salt flakes

Place the chocolate in a bain-marie and gently melt. Using an electric thermometer, bring the temperature of the chocolate to 55°C, then remove from the bain-marie and cool to 27–28°C by mixing constantly. Return to the bain-marie and carefully return to a temperature of 31–32°C. This will leave you with a tempered chocolate that, when set, will have a smooth, glossy finish.

Oil a shallow dish approximately 23 x 18cm and line with cling film, pressing into the corners. Pour in the chocolate and smooth over the top. Gently tap the dish on the work surface to extract any air, sprinkle with the chilli and sea salt and leave to set. Peel away the cling film, break into pieces and serve with rich coffee or use to decorate cakes.

MAYA'S CHOCOLATE-CHIP COOKIES

Every child should know how to make these. For the days when only cookies will do.

Takes 40 minutes / makes 15–20

200g butter, soft
50g unrefined caster sugar
120g unrefined light brown sugar
120g dark chocolate
  (drops or chopped)
175g oats
200g self-raising flour

Heat the oven to 180°C/gas mark 4. Line a baking sheet with baking parchment.

Cream together the butter and sugars, stir in the chocolate and oats, then finally add the flour and blend.

Roll the mixture by hand into 20–25 even-sized small balls. Flatten them slightly with the palm of your hand and place on the baking sheet, giving them enough room to spread when cooking. Bake in the oven for 15–20 minutes. Once golden and cooked, cool on a wire rack and, if not eaten at once, store in an airtight container.

The chocolate tree's scientific name, theobroma cacao, *comes from* theobroma, *or 'food of the gods' in Greek and* cacao, *from the Olmec word* kakawa.

'My door, slightly open, emits a hot scent of baking and sweetness.'

VIANNE'S HOT CHOCOLATE

So many people have asked me what Vianne puts in her chocolate. The answer varies, of course, depending on your favourites – but this is the classic recipe, passed down from Montezuma with only a few variations; rich, sweet and with just a little chilli kick . . .

Takes 15 minutes / serves 2

500ml full-fat milk
½ cinnamon stick
1 chilli, halved and deseeded,
  heat to choice
100g dark chocolate, broken
  into small even-sized pieces

unrefined brown sugar, to taste
Cognac, Amaretto, Cointreau
  or Tia Maria
100ml whipped double cream
½ teaspoon cocoa powder, or
  grated chocolate

Heat the milk in a saucepan with the cinnamon stick and chilli. Bring to a shivering simmer. Remove from the heat and add the chocolate to the milk. Blend until it melts. Add sugar to taste and leave to infuse for 10 minutes.

Reheat to a simmer, strain and pour into mugs. Add a dash of your favourite liqueur for a more grown-up taste, or top with whipped cream, a dusting of cocoa or grated chocolate.

When the seventeenth-century Bishop of Chiapas banned chocolate during church services, he was poisoned by his congregation – with a laced cup of hot chocolate.

JOE'S BLACKBERRY BROWNIES

Joe (and my grandfather) would have insisted on picking his own blackberries. Now you can buy them from supermarkets, of course; but somehow, those blackberries don't taste the same as when they're scavenged from a piece of wasteland or picked from the side of a country road . . .

Takes 50 minutes / serves 8

120g dark chocolate, broken into
  small, even-sized pieces
120g butter
2 eggs
225g unrefined caster sugar
110g self-raising flour
150g blackberries

Heat the oven to 180°C/gas mark 4. Line an 18 x 18cm shallow baking tin with baking parchment.

Place the chocolate and butter in a large saucepan over a very low heat and melt, mixing frequently. Remove from the heat when melted, then whisk the eggs and add them to the mixture, along with the sugar and flour. Mix until smooth. Add 100g of the blackberries and gently stir.

Pour into the prepared baking tin. Scatter the remaining blackberries on top and cook in the middle of the oven for 30 minutes until just set and a crust has formed on top. Leave to cool, then cut into 25–30 squares.

GÂTEAU MANON BLANC

This innocent-looking white chocolate-vanilla cake hides a multitude of mortal sins. For plausible denial, eat the evidence.

Takes 2½ hours / serves 8–10

Cake
butter for greasing tin
250g butter
150g white chocolate, broken
  into small, even-sized pieces
250ml milk
1 vanilla pod, seeds
  scraped out
250g self-raising flour
¼ tsp baking powder
270g unrefined caster sugar
3 eggs, beaten

Icing
100g white chocolate, broken
  into small, even-sized pieces
300g cream cheese
100g icing sugar

Heat the oven to 160°C/gas mark 3. Grease a 20cm loose-bottomed non-stick cake tin.

In a small saucepan, place the butter, white chocolate, milk and vanilla seeds. Heat gently and stir until melted. In a mixing bowl, place the flour, baking powder and sugar, then mix well. Pour in the melted chocolate mixture and the eggs, and quickly combine until smooth.

Pour into the prepared tin, place in the middle of the oven and bake for 1 hour. Check that the cake is cooked by inserting a knife into the centre – it should come out clean. If it doesn't, cook for a little longer. Once removed from the oven, rest the cake for 5 minutes and then remove it from the tin and leave to cool on a cooling wire.

To make the icing, melt the white chocolate in a bain-marie, then whisk together the cream cheese and icing sugar. Pour in the melted white chocolate and whisk quickly; if needed, chill the mix until it has a spreadable consistency. Put the cake on a serving plate, then, using a palette knife, cover all over with the icing.

In the eighteenth century, French philosopher Marquis de Sade was once imprisoned for using chocolate to mask the flavour of the drugs he liked to administer in secret to women.

AZTEC GOLD

I like to leave the peel intact for this, my favourite chocolate treat. Fran likes to remove it. You can decide for yourself which you prefer; either way, the sticky, half-crystallized orange strips are perfect with a half-coating of dark and bittersweet chocolate. As far as I'm concerned, this is what oranges were made for . . .

Takes 2½ hours, plus 24 hours' drying / makes approx. 100

5 large unwaxed oranges
500g unrefined caster sugar
175g dark chocolate, broken into
   small, even-sized pieces

Peel the oranges and cut into thin strips approximatley 5cm long and 6mm wide. Place in a large pan and cover with water. Bring to the boil, and then simmer for 5 minutes. Drain and return the strips to the pan with 1 litre of fresh water, then bring to the boil and simmer for 1 hour. Add the sugar, stir, bring back to a simmer and cook for 30 minutes. In this time the syrup should evaporate, leaving the orange strips coated in sticky syrup. Remove and arrange on a sheet of baking parchment and leave in a warm, dry place to dry out for 24 hours – an airing cupboard is best.

When ready, melt the chocolate in a bain-marie, dip one end of each orange strip into the chocolate, place on another sheet of baking parchment and leave to set.

Eat within the month.

Chocolate was the ultimate Aztec man's drink, consumed by leaders, warriors and sacrificial victims. Conquered people, on the other hand, had to pay the Aztec tribute in cacao beans.

MOCHA MOUSSE WITH AMARETTI

This easy-to-make mocha dessert works beautifully for dinner parties. Just make sure you make a few extra to enjoy after your guests have gone . . .

Takes 2½ hours / serves 6

100ml double cream
4 tbsp fresh espresso coffee
200g dark chocolate, grated
4 eggs, separated
100g amaretti biscuits, crushed

Gently warm the cream, then remove from the heat and add the espresso and chocolate. Stir until all the chocolate has dissolved and is blended. Whisk the egg yolks, then slowly add to the warm chocolate mixture and blend. Whisk the egg whites into stiff peaks. Add half to the chocolate and mix well, then add the remaining egg whites and blend.

Spoon into individual serving pots, filling halfway. Sprinkle in a layer of the crushed amaretti, then top with another layer of the mousse and finally finish with another dusting of amaretti. Chill for a minimum of 2 hours.

Chocolate is commonly believed to be an aphrodisiac and was used by Casanova, who mixed it with champagne.

'. . . the air is perfumed with bewildering scents . . .'

PANETTONE PAIN PERDU

How do you improve on a classic? By adding chocolate, of course. My grandmother used to make a version of this, which she called *pain perdu* – a traditional way of using day-old French bread. It works even better with Panettone – although, let's face it, whoever lets Panettone go stale in the first place?

Takes 1 hour 10 minutes / serves 4–6

200ml milk	*2 eggs*
25g cocoa powder	*150ml double cream*
250g Panettone	*2 tbsp unrefined caster sugar*
50g butter, soft	*icing sugar, for dusting*

Grease a 1-litre shallow, ovenproof baking dish with some of the butter.

Warm the milk, add the cocoa and mix to blend. Slice the Panettone and spread with the remaining butter. Cut each slice in half and arrange in the dish.

Whisk the eggs, cream, sugar and warm chocolate milk together and pour over the Panettone, pressing down with a spatula so the Panettone absorbs the liquid. Leave to sit for 30 minutes.

Heat the oven to 160°C/gas mark 3.

Fill a roasting tin with 3cm of hot water, place the baking dish in it and bake in the middle of the oven for 30 minutes; the pudding should be golden on top and just set. Dust with icing sugar and serve with chocolate ice cream.

PEANUT CHOCOLATE BRITTLE

Fran likes to use unsalted peanuts for this recipe, although I rather like the salty kind . . .

Takes 45 minutes / serves 12

200g peanuts, unsalted
200g granulated sugar
100g chocolate, broken into
  small, even-sized pieces

Heat the oven to 150°C/gas mark 2.

Place the peanuts on a baking tray and cook for 10 minutes until a light golden brown. Remove from the oven and set to one side.

Put the sugar in a heavy-based non-stick saucepan over a medium heat and shake until all the sugar has melted evenly into a golden-coloured caramel. Do not leave it, as it burns very quickly. Add the peanuts and stir quickly with a wooden spoon. Pour out on to a sheet of baking parchment, flatten and leave to cool.

When the brittle is completely cool, melt the chocolate in a bain-marie and spread over the top of the brittle. Leave to set. Or, if you prefer, melt a small amount of contrasting chocolate as well and then quickly drizzle both of them 'Jackson Pollock-style' over the top and leave to set. Cut into small chunks, using a sharp knife. This works well on its own or with ice cream.

SPICED NIPPLES OF VENUS

Nipples of Venus, or *Capezzoli di Venere*, have been claimed as an Italian confection, but they have been known in France and throughout Europe since the eighteenth century. There are many variations on the original recipe, which sometimes includes candied chestnuts or marzipan, but I like this subtly spiced version with cinnamon ganache. There is some argument over whether the 'nipples' should be dark or light: the original recipe says that the chocolate should be dark, with a white nipple, but I think both versions are equally attractive. After all, beauty comes in all shades . . .

Takes 2 hours, plus setting / makes approx. 40

Filling
300g dark or milk chocolate, broken
   into small, even-sized pieces
200ml double cream
½ tsp cinnamon

Dipping
200g dark chocolate, broken into
   small, even-sized pieces
50g white chocolate, broken into
   small, even-sized pieces

For the filling, place your chosen chocolate in a bain-marie and gently melt. Warm the cream and add to the melted chocolate along with the cinnamon, mixing until evenly blended. Leave to cool and set for 2 hours.

Once set, the mixture will need to be beaten to a piping consistency; using an electric whisk, mix until the chocolate cream is smooth and stiff enough to hold its shape. Put the mixture in a piping bag fitted with a plain 1–2cm nozzle. Line a large tray with baking parchment and pipe out little nipples, then place them in the fridge to set hard.

Melt the dark chocolate in a bain-marie, and in a separate one also melt the white chocolate.

To dip the nipples, insert a small fork into the flat underside of each one and dip to coat all over in the darker chocolate, followed by just the tips in the white chocolate. After a few dippings the melted white chocolate will have threads of dark chocolate marbled through it and each nipple will start to take on its own individual dipped effect. Place each one back on the baking parchment and leave to set. Repeat until all are coated.

MAYA GOLD CHOCOLATE POPCORN

This easy-to-make treat celebrates the two most venerated foods of the Mayan and Aztec culture – maize and chocolate – for a deliciously salty-sweet combination.

Takes 3 hours / serves 8

50g maize or popcorn
150g dark chocolate, broken into
  small, even-sized pieces
150g milk chocolate, broken into
  small, even-sized pieces
100ml double cream
1 tsp crystal sea salt

Line a 22 x 12cm loaf tin with cling film.

If using maize, heat it in a popcorn machine, the microwave or in a pan over a medium heat until the maize bursts into popcorn.

In two separate bain-maries, melt the dark and milk chocolate. Then, when melted, add half the cream to each and quickly blend in until the mixture stiffens. Pour both on to the popcorn, then add ½ teaspoon of the crystal sea salt and mix until all the popcorn is coated.

Place in the lined loaf tin and press down, then sprinkle the top with the remaining salt. Put in the fridge to cool and set for at least 2½ hours. Remove from the tin, peel away the cling film and slice with a large, sharp knife.

Mayan emperors were often buried with jars of chocolate by their sides. The Mayan symbol for the cacao pod was a heart.

'We perch on our stools like New York barflies, a
cup of chocolate each. Anouk has hers with crème
Chantilly and chocolate curls; I drink mine hot
and black, stronger than espresso.'

CARDAMOM HOT CHOCOLATE

Cardamom and chocolate work wonderfully well together to give this version of the classic drink a subtle, sophisticated flavour. I like to crank up the cardamom taste – just add a couple of cracked seed pods and let the spices work their magic . . .

Takes 15 minutes / serves 2

500ml full-fat milk
4 cardamom seeds, crushed
100g dark chocolate, grated
unrefined brown sugar, to taste
100ml whipped cream

Heat the milk in a saucepan. Add the crushed cardamom seeds, chocolate and sugar to taste, then bring to a shivering simmer. Remove from the heat and leave to infuse for 10 minutes.

Reheat to a simmer, strain and pour into mugs, topped with whipped cream and a dusting of cocoa powder or grated chocolate.

ROSETTE'S CHOCOLATE FRIDGE CAKE

This recipe is so easy that even a child can make it – in fact, I know from experience that the task of destroying biscuits by hitting them with a rolling pin can become so popular with children that it's hard to make them understand that it isn't always necessary. There are many variations on this basic recipe – here we've used raisins and pecans, but almonds and cherries work well too, as do sultanas and orange peel.

Takes 2½ hours / serves 12

250g digestive biscuits
300g dark or milk chocolate,
*   broken into small,*
*   even-sized pieces*

100g butter
100g golden syrup
100g raisins
100g pecans, chopped

Line a 30 x 20cm shallow baking tray with baking parchment.

Place the biscuits in a plastic bag and bash with a rolling pin. Melt the chocolate, butter and golden syrup in a bain-marie, mixing until smooth. Remove from the heat, add the digestive biscuits, raisins and pecans, and mix well, coating everything in the chocolate syrup.

Put the mixture into the prepared tray, push down and flatten the top. Place in the fridge to set for 2 hours. Remove from the tray, dust with icing sugar or cocoa powder and cut into 12 squares (or hearts, or stars, if you prefer).

INDEX

ACKNOWLEDGEMENTS

Chocolate is enjoyed by all, be it in a small square or a whole bar! It would not have been possible for this book to arrive in your home without the help of a great working team – and, in both small and large contributions, each and every person has been equally important in making this totally delicious and indulgent book.

It is our pleasure to thank you all. Especially: the genius Marianne Velmans, who conceived the project; Rebecca Wright and Bella Whittington, who guided, edited and organized the book into its final fantastic form; Lisa Horton, who designed the book while working closely with the master food photographer Philip Webb and his adept technical assistant Simon Reed; Pene Parker, for gathering props for us to present this fine chocolate feast; Ottilie Sandford, who helped me in the hot summer days to prepare each recipe for this book. Thank you also to our agents, Anna Power and Peter Robinson, who help keep the paperwork in order!

Finally, thanks to one of London's finest female chocolate shop proprietors, Chantal Coady of Rococo chocolates, who provided us with a constant flow of Valrhona chocolate!

ABOUT THE AUTHORS

Joanne Harris is the author of *Chocolat* (made into an Oscar-nominated film in 2000, with Juliette Binoche and Johnny Depp), and ten more bestselling novels. Her work is published in over fifty countries and has sold an estimated 30 million copies worldwide. She lives in Yorkshire with her family, plays bass in a band first formed when she was sixteen, works in a shed in her garden, likes musical theatre and old sci-fi, drinks rather too much caffeine, spends far too much time online and occasionally dreams of faking her own death and going to live in Hawaii.

Fran Warde's career has been fuelled by a passion for food. Trained as a chef, she worked at the Café Royal, on an Australian prawn trawler, ran her own cookery school and then moved into food styling and food writing. She was the food editor at *Red* magazine and is the author of *Ginger Pig Meat Book*, *Ginger Pig Farmhouse Cookbook*, *Food for Friends*, *Eat Drink Live* and *30 Minute Italian*. She lives in West London with her husband and two children.